the **CONCERT PERFORMER SERIES**

Joplin

The Entertainer

Cover photography: Copyright © 1999 David Ward/Panoramic Images, Chicago
All Rights Reserved.

Project editor: Peter Pickow

Copyright © 1999 by Amsco Publications,
A Division of Music Sales Corporation, New York

All rights reserved. No part of this publication may be
reproduced in any form or by any electronic or mechanical means,
including information storage and retrieval systems,
without permission in writing from the publisher.

Order No. AM 949817
International Standard Book Number: 0.8256.1748.0

Exclusive Distributors:
Music Sales Corporation
257 Park Avenue South, New York, NY 10010 USA
Music Sales Limited
8/9 Frith Street, London W1V 5TZ England
Music Sales Pty. Limited
120 Rothschild Street, Rosebery, Sydney, NSW 2018, Australia

Printed in the United States of America by
Vicks Lithograph and Printing Corporation

Amsco Publications
New York/London/Paris/Sydney/Copenhagen/Madrid

The Entertainer

Scott Joplin